Don't Stand in Front of a Palace or Behind a Horse:

An Illustrated Book of South Indian Proverbs

Expanded Second Edition

By

Tonse N. K. Raju, MD.

AUCTOREM
H O U S E

Auctorem House
276 5th Ave, Ste 704-2591
New York, NY 10001
www.auctoremhouse.com
Phone: 1 888-332-7718

Published by Auctorem House: 12/03/2025

ISBN: 978-1-965687-88-8(sc)
ISBN: 978-1-965687-89-5(e)

Library of Congress Control Number: 2025905432

Table of Contents

....
....

Preface

A proverb in your speech is like chutney with your rice, so goes a South Indian saying. This book serves a bit of literary chutney from India. It is a collection of popular proverbs from Kannada, a South Indian language with a rich literary history and cultural heritage. Kannada is the mother tongue of nearly 80 million people worldwide and the official language of the Indian state of Karnataka.

Like people from other ancient cultures, Indians regularly use proverbs in their conversation. Growing up in India, I was always impressed by my grandfather's narrative style. Mixing proverbs and similes to perfection, he could tell a story or debate an issue so dramatically that his listeners seldom forgot the encounter. This trait, however, is fast disappearing in the sterilized, civil tongues of urban India, as it is in other modern societies. Perhaps, reading books on proverbs might remedy our collective amnesia; this is one of the reasons for this book. Other reasons are as follows.

Proverbs tend to fade away with time, especially if not committed to pen and paper—or to laptops, these days. Each generation must therefore strive to save the gems of their time for future generations. The palest ink is better than the best memory, according to a Chinese proverb.

These proverbs will introduce the non-Kannada reader to one aspect of Indian culture. One can narrow cultural gaps by taking small steps, and proverbs are a fun way to achieve this goal. The reader will notice that these proverbs not only emanate the essence of the Indian soil they sprang from but also reflect universal themes.

Perhaps proverbs originated as spontaneous, succinct phrases uttered by ordinary people in moments of distress, ecstasy, or genuine wickedness. Thus, they remain the authentic voice of the general public—perhaps more relevant than that of God. Brimming with wit and wisdom, these Kannada proverbs, too, reflect the true grit of the commoner. Children and grandchildren in all foreign lands—particularly those who might have missed their grandfathers' eloquences—may find these pages worth reading. In the Appendix, I have explained the Indian context for some of the proverbs, for without which, their meanings might remain obscure. I have included the original versions of the proverbs in Kannada font to enable Kannada readers to compare them with the respective translations.

I am very grateful to Arthur Baltazar for enriching this book with his superb cartoons. I thank Sharat Raju for an excellent editing job. Others who corrected the manuscript at various stages: Drs. Kristine McCulloch, Mrinalini Rao, Ralph Strohl, and Tanzeema Hossain—I thank them all.

Tonse N.K. Raju, MD
www.tonseraju.com

Preface to the Second Edition

In this second edition, I have added 49 proverbs bringing the total to 300. The first edition was published by 1st Books Library, later reprinted by Author House. This second edition is being published by Auctorem House and Boundless Book Publishers. I thank the staff from these entities who helped in bringing this volume to print.

To the memories of

Kodavooru Padmanabha Aithal,
my grandfather,
who taught me how to tell a story,

and to

Tonse Narayana Udupa and
Lakshmi Udupa,
My parents for instilling in me,
the fundamental values of life.

Adolescence-Age

Even a pig appears pretty in adolescence.

ಪ್ರಾಯ ಬಂದಾಗ ಹಂದಿ ಸಹಾ ಚಂದ.

A budding leaf mocks the fallen foliage.

ಹಣ್ಣೆಲೆ ಉದುರುವಾಗ ಚಿಗುರೆಲೆ ನಕ್ಕಿತಂತೆ.

A youth's sprouting mustache blinds him to the world.

ಮೀಸೆ ಬಂದವನಿಗೆ ದೇಶ ಕಾಣದು.

Alliances (shifting)

For three pancakes, I side with mother-
in-law. For six, I will side with daughter-
in-law.

ಮೂರು ದೋಸೆಗೆ ಅತ್ತೆಯ ಕಡೆ, ಆರು ದೋಸೆಗೆ
ಸೊಸೆಯ ಕಡೆ

Anger

A poor man's anger leads to a broken jaw.

ಬಡವನ ಕೋಪ ದವಡೆಗೆ ಮೂಲ.

Smart men control their anger.

ಜಾಣರಿಗೆ ಕೋಪ ಕಡಿಮೆ.

If you get angry at the stream [of water], don't stop cleaning your butt.

ಕೆರೆ ಮೇಲೆ ಕೋಪಿಸ್ಕೊಂಡು ತಿಕ ತೊಳೆಯದು ಬಿಟ್ರಂತೆ.

A nose cut off in anger will not grow back upon becoming calm.

ಕೋಪದಲ್ಲಿ ಕುಯ್ದ ಮೂಗು ಶಾಂತವಾದ ಮೇಲೆ ಬರುವುದೇ?

City-Village

Our village monkey reigns as a king in the city. [1]

ನಮ್ಮ ಹಳ್ಳಿ ಕೋತಿ, ನಗರದಲ್ಲಿ ರಾಜ.

Common sense

Even absolute truths must be verified.

ಎಲ್ಲಾ ಸತ್ಯವನ್ನೂ ಪರೀಕ್ಷಿಸಿ ನೋಡಬೇಕು.

Check the horse before riding, the soil before sowing.

ಹತ್ತೋಕೆ ಮೊದಲು ಕುದುರೆ ನೋಡು,
ಬಿತ್ತೋಕೆ ಮೊದಲು ಹೊಲ ನೋಡು.

Don't lament your hardships with the tax collector.

ಸುಂಕದವನ ಮುಂದೆ ಸುಖ ದುಃಖ ಹೇಳಬೇಡ.

To get your work done, don't hesitate to salute even the mule.

ಕಾರ್ಯಾವಾಸಿ ಕತ್ತೆ ಕಾಲು ಕಟ್ಟು.

Polluted environment results in catastrophes

ಪರಿಸರದ ಮಾಲಿನ್ಯ ವಿನಾಶಕ್ಕೆ ಕಾರಣ.

The needle may be golden; do you prick eyes with it?

ಚಿನ್ನದ ಸೂಜಿ ಅಂತ ಕಣ್ಣು ಚುಚ್ಚಿಕೊಂಡಾರೇ?

Use a needle to remove a thorn.

ಮುಳ್ಳನ್ನು ಮುಳ್ಳಿನಿಂದಲೇ ತೆಗಿ.

Avoid a swinging stick; live for a hundred years.

ಬೀಸೋ ದೊಣ್ಣೆ ತಪ್ಪಿದರೆ ಸೂರುವರ್ಷ ಆಯಸ್ಸು.

Complaint

Even a mother does not feed her son who isn't crying.

ಅಳದ ಮಗುವಿಗೆ ಅಮ್ಮನೂ ಹಾಲು ಕೊಡಳು.

Cooperation

A clap can only happen when both palms meet.

ಎರಡೂ ಕೈ ತಟ್ಟಿದರೇ ಚಪ್ಪಾಳೆ.

You need both ears to hold the spectacles on the face.

ಎರಡೂ ಕಿವಿ ಇದ್ದರೇ ಕನ್ನಡಕ ನಿಂತೀತು.

Critic

A dog's bark doesn't insult the heavens.

ನಾಯಿ ಬೊಗಳಿದರೆ ಸ್ವರ್ಗ ಹಾಳಾದೀತೇ!

Rain drenches but not the sunshine.

ಮಳೆ ಬಿಸಿಲನ್ನು ಮುಟ್ಟದು.

Salute the critic.

ವಿಮರ್ಶಕನಿಗೆ ನಮಸ್ಕಾರ.

A lucky man has a hundred critics.

ಅದೃಷ್ಟವಂತನಿಗೆ ನೂರು ಜನರ ಟೀಕೆ.

As futile as spitting at the sun.

ಸೂರ್ಯನಿಗೆ ಉಗಿದಂತೆ.

Cry Wolf

Who can cry for a man that dies each day?

ದಿನಾ ಸಾಯುವವನಿಗೆ ಅಳುವವರು ಯಾರು?

Cunning/Outwitting

The monkey ate the butter but wiped it on the goat's mouth.

ಕೋತಿ ಬೆಣ್ಣೆ ತಿಂದು ಆಡಿನ ಬಾಯಿಗೆ ಒರೆಸಿತಂತೆ!

If mom can slide under the carpet, the daughter can slide under the floor.

ತಾಯಿ ಚಾಪೆಯಡಿಯಲ್ಲಿ ನುಸುಳಿದರೆ ಮಗಳು ರಂಗೋಲೆಯಡಿಯಲ್ಲಿ ನುಸುಳಿದಳಂತೆ!

If you reveal your fingers [to him], he will swallow your whole arm.

ಬೆರಳು ತೋರಿಸಿದರೆ ಹಸ್ತ ನುಂಗಿದನಂತೆ!

Mouth filled with sugar; heart filled with venom.

ಬಾಯಿಯಲ್ಲಿ ಬೆಲ್ಲ ಎದೆಯಲ್ಲಿ ನೀಚತನ.

Deceptive Appearances

Even anthills shelter snakes.

ಹುತ್ತದೊಳಗೂ ಹಾವಿರುತ್ತದೆ.

Small seeds spawn tall trees.

ಬೀಜ ಸಣ್ಣದಾದರೂ ಮರ ದೊಡ್ಡದು.

Even the blackest cow yields white milk.

ಹಸು ಕಪ್ಪಾದರೂ ಹಾಲು ಬಿಳಿ.

A crow is a crow—not a nightingale.

ಕಾಗೆ ಕಾಗೆಯೇ, ಕೋಗಿಲೆ ಕೋಗಿಲೆಯೇ.

Even the most crooked sugarcane contains sweet juice.

ಕಬ್ಬು ಡೊಂಕಾದರೇನು, ಅದರ ಸವಿ ಡೊಂಕೇ?

Sugarcane may be sweet, but not its root.

ಕಬ್ಬು ಸಿಹಿಯಿದ್ದರೂ ಅದರ ಬೇರು ಸಿಹಿಯೇ?

By looking at an anthill, you cannot guess the kind of snake that lies within.

ಯಾವ ಹುತ್ತದಲ್ಲಿ ಎಂಥಾ ಹಾವೋ!

Lotuses bloom in dirty ponds.

ಕೆಸರಿನಲ್ಲೂ ಕಮಲ ಅರಳುತ್ತದೆ.

All that is white is not milk.

ಬೆಳ್ಳಗಿರುವುವುದೆಲ್ಲಾ ಹಾಲಲ್ಲ.

Sweet grapes, sour wine.

ದ್ರಾಕ್ಷಿ ಸಿಹಿ, ದ್ರಾಕ್ಷಾರಸ ಹುಳಿ.

A golden needle's prick still hurts.

ಚಿನ್ನದ ಸೂಜಿಯಾದರೂ ಚುಚ್ಚಿದರೆ ನೋಯದೇ?

From far away, all hills appear smooth.

ದೂರದ ಬೆಟ್ಟ ನುಣ್ಣಗೆ.

Even a three-feet vein may yield six-feet melons.

ಗಿಡ ಮೂರು ಮೊಳ, ಕಾಯಿ ಆರು ಮೋಳ.

Small size, large fame.

ಮೂರ್ತಿ ಚಿಕ್ಕದಾದರೂ ಕೀರ್ತಿ ದೊಡ್ಡದು.

Even if you trust a thief, don't trust a dwarf. [2]

ಕಳ್ಳನನ್ನು ನಂಬಿದರೂ ಕುಳ್ಳನನ್ನು ನಂಬಬೇಡ.

Beware of [people with] red hairs or 'cat's-eyes.' [2]

ಕೆಂಪು ಕೂದಲಿರುವವರನ್ನೂ ಕೊತ್ತಿ ಕಣ್ಣು
ಇರುವವರನ್ನೂ ನಂಬಬೇಡ.[2]

Even a tiny spark can burn the whole forest.

ಕಿಡಿ ಸಣ್ಣದಾದರೂ ಕಾಡೆಲ್ಲವನ್ನು ಸುಡಬಲ್ಲದು.

Sunshine during monsoon and sweet talks of a smiling man cannot be trusted.

ಮಳೆಗಾಲದ ಬಿಸಿಲನ್ನು, ನಗೆಗಾರನ ಮಾತನ್ನು
ನಂಬಬೇಡ.

Doctors and Patients

An old patient is better than a new doctor.

ಹೊಸ ವೈದ್ಯನಿಗಿಂತ ಹಳೇ ರೋಗಿಯೇ ಮೇಲು.

Don't lie to your doctor or your lawyer.

ವೈದ್ಯನ ಹತ್ತಿರ ವಕೀಲನ ಹತ್ತಿರ ಸುಳ್ಳು ಹೇಳಬೇಡ.

Eagerness

Do not stitch the baby-cap before the baby's birth.

ಕೂಸು ಹುಟ್ಟುವ ಮೊದಲೇ ಕುಲಾವಿ ಹೊಲಿದಂತೆ!

Don't count the chicks before the eggs hatch.

ಮರಿ ಹುಟ್ಟುವ ಮೊದಲೇ ಮೊಟ್ಟೆಗಳನ್ನು ಎಣಿಸಬೇಡ.

Effort/Self-help/ Laziness

Idle in the stable, even a royal horse becomes a mule.

ಲಾಯದಲ್ಲಿ ಕಟ್ಟಿದ ರಾಯರ ಕುದುರೆ ಬರ್ತಾ ಬರ್ತಾ

ಕತ್ತೆ ಆಯ್ತಂತೆ!

To work is heaven.

ಕಾಯಕವೇ ಕೈಲಾಸ.

A frog's croak cannot fill a pond.

ಕಪ್ಪೆ ಕೂಗಿದರೆ ಕೊಳ ತುಂಬೀತೇ?

The nectar of laziness is poison.

ಆಲಸ್ಯಂ ಅಮೃತಂ ವಿಷಂ.

Mantras don't make mangoes drop from the tree.

ಮಂತ್ರಿಸಿದರೆ ಮಾವಿನ ಕಾಯಿ ಬೀಳುವುದೇ?

Even to stammer you must try to speak first. Even to stumble you must try to walk first.

ತೊದಲ ಬೇಕಾದರೂ ನುಡಿಯಬೇಕು,
ಎಡವಬೇಕಾದರೂ ನಡೆಯಬೇಕು.

A pond fills a drop at a time; a barn fills a grain at a time.

ಹನಿ ಹನಿ ಕೂಡಿದರೆ ಹಳ್ಳ, ತೆನೆ ತೆನೆ ಕೋಡಿದರೆ
ಬಳ್ಳ.

If you are thirsty, find a river; the river won't flow to you.

ಬಾಯಾರಿದರೆ ನದಿಗೆ ಹೋಗು; ನದಿ ನಿನ್ನ ಬಳಿಗೆ
ಬಾರದು.

Hands dirtied from work fill your mouth.
ಕೈಕೆಸರಾದರೆ ಬಾಯಿ ಮೊಸರು.

If you wish for heaven, you must die for it.

ಸ್ವತಃ ಸಾಯದೇ ಸ್ವರ್ಗ ಸಿಗದು.

How far can we push up and support the butt of a man who wants to climb a coconut tree?

ತೆಂಗಿನ ಮರ ಹತ್ತುವವನ ತಿಕ ಎಲ್ಲಿ ತನಕ ಎತ್ತಿ
ಹಿಡಿಯಲಾಗುವುದು?

Experience

Pain increases knowledge.

ಬಿದ್ದ ಮೇಲೆ ಬುದ್ಧಿ ಬಂತು.

Grandmothers know how to cough.[3]

ಅಜ್ಜಿಗೆ ಕೆಮ್ಮು ಕಲಿಸಬೇಕೇ?

Only by running will you have muscle aches.

ಓಡುವವನೇ ಬಲ್ಲ ತೊಡೆ ನೋವ.

False Hope

Do not wish for the reflection of a pot of gold in the mirror.

ಕನ್ನಡಿಯೊಳಗಿನ ಗಂಟಿನಂತೆ.

Fear

For the faint at heart, even a rope looks like a snake.

ಹೆದರಿದವನಿಗೆ ಹಗ್ಗವೂ ಹಾವು.

Fickle Mind

Untamed minds behave like a bunch of frogs on a weighing balance.

ಕಪ್ಪೆತೂಕ ಮಾಡಿದ ಹಾಗೆ.

Formality

Water is holy only when it flows from a conch.

ನೀರು ಶಂಖದಿಂದ ಬಂದಾಗಲೇ ತೀರ್ಥವಾಗುವುದು.

Friendship

Never deceive a friend

ಗೆಳೆಯನಿಗೆ ಮೋಸ ಮಾಡಬೇಡ.

God

When in trouble, pray.

ಸಂಕಟ ಬಂದರೆ ವೆಂಕಟರಮಣ.

Six attempts are mine. The seventh attempt is that of God.

ಆರು ಯತ್ನ ನನ್ನದು, ಏಳನೇಯದು ದೈವೇಚ್ಛೆ.

The world is my temple.

ಪ್ರಪಂಚವೇ ನನ್ನ ದೇಗುಲ.

God gives you the boon, the priest takes it away.

ದೇವರು ಕೊಟ್ಟರೂ ಪೂಜಾರಿ ಬಿಡ.

Meditation begets knowledge.

ಧ್ಯಾನದಿಂದ ಬುದ್ಧಿ ಬಂತು.

Don't we know the dark secrets of our own God?

ನಮ್ಮ ದೇವರ ಸತ್ಯ ನಮಗೆ ತಿಳಿಯದೇ?

Goodwill

If you get pregnant out of goodwill, you may not find a place to deliver.

ದಾಕ್ಷಿಣ್ಯಕ್ಕೆ ಬಸಿರಾದರೆ ಹೆರಲು ತಾವಿಲ್ಲ.

Donated wealth stays with you; hidden wealth goes to others.

ಕೊಟ್ಟದ್ದು ತನಗೆ ಬಚ್ಚಿಟ್ಟದ್ದು ಪರರಿಗೆ.

Lock your house, open your mind.

ಮನೆ ಬಾಗಿಲಿಗೆ ಬೀಗ ಹಾಕು, ಮನದ ಬಾಗಿಲನ್ನು ತೆರೆದಿಡು.

Gossip

A Story has no feet.

ಕತೆಗೆ ಕಾಲಿಲ್ಲ.

Gossip wanders.

ಹರಟೆ ಹಾರಾಡುತ್ತದೆ.

Greed

Greed is a bottomless pit.

ದುರಾಸೆ ಬುಡವಿಲ್ಲ ಹೊಂಡ.

Fervent desire never dies.

ಆಸೆಗೆ ಸಾವಿಲ್ಲ.

Habit (Nature)

The dog's tail is forever bent.

ನಾಯಿಯ ಬಾಲ ಯಾವಾಗಲೂ ಡೊಂಕು.

Even in the king's court, a dog will run after a bone.

ನಾಯಿ ಅರಮನೆಯಲ್ಲೂ ಮೂಳೆಯ ಹಿಂದೆ
ಓಡುತ್ತದೆ.

Happiness/Sadness

Happiness is youth, melancholy is
senility.

ಸಂತೋಷವೇ ಯೌವನ, ಚಿಂತೆಯೇ ಮುಪ್ಪು.

Hell/Heaven

No mercy in hell; no death in heaven.

ನರಕದಲ್ಲಿ ಕರುಣೆಯಿಲ್ಲ, ಸ್ವರ್ಗದಲ್ಲಿ ಮರಣವಿಲ್ಲ

Hidden Talent

Best fruits hide behind the leaves.

ಎಲೆಮರೆಯ ಹಣ್ಣಿನಂತೆ.

Ash-covered coal burns the hottest.

ಬೂದಿ ಮುಚ್ಚಿದ ಕೆಂಡದಂತೆ.

Honesty

A cat is very honest if the milk is out of reach.

ಹಾಲು ಎಟುಕದಿದ್ದರೆ ಬೆಕ್ಕು ಪ್ರಾಮಾಣಿಕ.

Humility

If you can be a slave, you can become a king, too.

ಆಳಾಗಬಲ್ಲವನು ಅರಸನಾಗಬಲ್ಲ.

Husband/Wife

When husband and wife quarrel, the baby withers away.

ಗಂಡ ಹೆಂಡಿರ ಜಗಳದಲ್ಲಿ ಮಗು ಬಡವಾಯಿತು.

An angry husband finds a stone in the yogurt.

ಒಲ್ಲದ ಗಂಡನಿಗೆ ಮೊಸರಿನಲ್ಲಿ ಕಲ್ಲು ಸಿಕ್ಕಿತಂತೆ.

Husband and wife's quarrel lasts until they dine and sleep.

ಗಂಡ ಹೆಂಡಿರ ಜಗಳ ಉಂಡು ಮಲಗುವ ತನಕ.

Your lawn after the rain and your daughter after your son-in-law comes home, look alike.

ಮಳೆಬಂದ ಮರುದಿನ ಹೊಲವನ್ನು ನೋಡು;

ಅಳಿಯ ಬಂದ ಮರುದಿನ ಮಗಳನ್ನು ನೋಡು.

Ignorance

The spoon cannot taste how good the soup is.

ಸಾರಿನ ರುಚಿ ಸೌಟಿಗೇನು ಗೊತ್ತು?

Half learned person roars a lot.

ಅರ್ಧಕಲಿತವನ ಅಬ್ಬರ ಹೆಚ್ಚು.

Does the monkey know the value of diamonds?

ಮಂಗನ ಕೈಯಲ್ಲಿ ಮಾಣಿಕ್ಯವಿದ್ದಂತೆ.

There is no light without darkness.

ಕತ್ತಲಿಲ್ಲದೇ ಬೆಳಕಿಲ್ಲ.

Flood waters have no regard for flower gardens.

ಕೋಡಿ ನೀರಿಗೇನು ಗೊತ್ತು ವೃಂದಾವನದ ಚಂದ?

"Your tail has a hole," mocked the sieve at the needle.

"ನಿನ್ನ ಬಾಲದಲ್ಲಿ ತೂತಿದೆ" ಅಂತ ಸೂಜಿಯನ್ನು ನೋಡಿ ಜರಡಿ ನಕ್ಕಿತು.

Before mocking the dead fly in your neighbor's patio, make sure no dead rat lies in your basement.

ನೆರಮನೆಯ ಅಂಗಳದಲ್ಲಿ ನೊಣನೋಡಿ
ನಗುವವನು ತನ್ನ ಮನೆಯಲ್ಲಿ ಸತ್ತಿಲಿ ಇದೆಯೇ
ನೋಡಬೇಕು

Even the lamp's base has darkness.

ದೀಪದ ಕೆಳಗೂ ಕತ್ತಲೆ.

Ignorance is grief [4]

ಅಜ್ಞಾನವೇ ದುಃಖ.

Indecision

Don't place one leg on one boat, and the other on the other boat at the same time.

ಎರಡು ದೋಣಿಯ ಮೇಲೆ ಕಾಲಿಡಬೇಡ.

Jealousy

Jealousy is the root cause of destruction.

ಎಲ್ಲ ಕೆಡುಕಿಗೂ ಮೂಲ ಹೊಟ್ಟೆಕಿಚ್ಚು.

Most illnesses have cures; jealousy has no cure.

ವಿವಿಧ ರೋಗಗಳಿಗೆ ಮದ್ದಿವೆ, ಹೊಟ್ಟೆ ಉರಿಗೆ ಮದ್ದಿಲ್ಲ.

Karma (Fate)

A chef must eat what he cooks.

ಮಾಡಿದ್ದುಣ್ಣೋ ಮಹಾರಾಯ.

The one with peanuts has no teeth, the one who has teeth has no peanuts.

ಕಡಲೆ ಇದ್ದವನಿಗೆ ಹಲ್ಲಿಲ್ಲ, ಹಲ್ಲಿದ್ದವನಿಗೆ ಕಡಲೆಯಿಲ್ಲ.

If you eat salt, you will have to drink water.

ಉಪ್ಪುಂಡವನು ನೀರು ಕುಡಿಯಲೇಬೇಕು.

Hell has nine doors; heaven has only one.

ನರಕಕ್ಕೆ ಒಂಬತ್ತು ಬಾಗಿಲು, ಸ್ವರ್ಗಕ್ಕೆ ಒಂದೇ ಬಾಗಿಲು.

Kings and their Men

Don't stand in front of a palace or behind a horse.

ಅರಮನೆಯ ಮುಂದಿರಬೇಡ, ಕುದುರೆಯ
ಹಿಂದಿರಬೇಡ.

If the king gets angry (at you), emigrate.

ಅರಸ ಮುನಿದೊಡೆ ನಾಡೊಳಗಿರಬಾರದು.

As is the king, so are his subjects.

ಯಥಾರಾಜಾ ತಥಾ ಪ್ರಜಾ.

Don't build your house next to the palace.

ಅರಮನೆಯ ಬಳಿ ನೆರಮನೆ ಇರಬಾರದು.

Praise the king to his face, a son behind his back.

ಆರಸನನ್ನು ಮುಂದೆ ಹೊಗಳು, ಮಗನನ್ನು ಹಿಂದೆ ಹೊಗಳು.

The king can disagree, a serf must agree.

ರಾಜ ಅಲ್ಲ ಎನ್ನಬಹುದು, ಆಳು ಹೌದು ಎನ್ನಲೇಬೇಕು.

Life/Fate/Bad Luck

When [one's] end is near, even the mind goes crazy.

ವಿನಾಶಕಾಲೇ ವಿಪರೀತ ಬುದ್ಧಿ.

Naked at birth, naked at death.

ನಗ್ನ ಜನನ, ನಗ್ನ ಮರಣ.

It is better to live like a lion for one year than like a goat for a thousand.

ಕುರಿಯಂತೆ ಸಾವಿರ ವರ್ಷ ಬಾಳುವ ಬದಲು,

ಹುಲಿಯಂತೆ ಒಂದು ವರ್ಷ ಬಾಳುವುದು ಮೇಲು.

It is better to burn for a minute with satisfaction than to broil with desire forever.

ಆಸೆಯಲ್ಲಿ ಬೇಯುವ ಬದಲು ತೃಪ್ತಿಯಿಂದ ಉರಿಯುವುದು ಮೇಲು.

All stoves emit smoke.

ಎಲ್ಲಾ ಒಲೆಯಲ್ಲೂ ಹೊಗೆ.

Each family has a coughing grandmother. [3]

ಎಲ್ಲರಮನೆಯಲ್ಲೂ ಕೆಮ್ಮುವ ಅಜ್ಜಿ.

In the year of famine, we had an extra month of rainless summer.

ದುರ್ಭಿಕ್ಷದಲ್ಲಿ ಅಧಿಕಮಾಸ.

Pancake in every house has holes.

ಎಲ್ಲರ ಮನೆಯ ದೋಸೆಯೂ ತೂತು.

A hell on this earth is better than the heaven after death.

ಸತ್ತು ಸಿಗುವ ಸ್ವರ್ಗಕ್ಕಿಂತ ಬದುಕಿ ಪಡೆವ
ನರಕವೇ ಲೇಸು.

Even the mighty fire becomes a heap of ash.

ಉರಿಯುವ ಬೆಂಕಿಯೂ ಬೂದಿಯ
ರಾಶಿಯಾಗುತ್ತದೆ.

A snake charmer meets his death through the snake.

ಹಾವಾಡಿಗನಿಗೆ ಹಾವಿನಿಂದಲೇ ಮರಣ.

Limits / Limitations

Don't stretch your legs beyond the mattress.

ಹಾಸಿಗೆ ಇದ್ದಷ್ಟೇ ಕಾಲು ಚಾಚು.

"The dancing floor is crooked," complained the blind dancer.

ಕುಣಿಯಲಾರದ ಕುರುಡು ನರ್ತಕಿ ನೆಲ ಡೊಂಕು
ಎಂದಳಂತೆ.

Our preacher has more spit than sermon.

ಮಂತ್ರಕ್ಕಿಂತ ಉಗುಳು ಜಾಸ್ತಿ.

Living Dangerously

Like the tongue living among the sharp teeth.

ಹಲ್ಲಿನ ನಡುವೆ ನಾಲಿಗೆಯಂತೆ.

Don't lick honey from the knife's edge.

ಕತ್ತಿಗೆ ಮೆತ್ತಿಕೊಂಡ ಜೇನು ನೆಕ್ಕಬೇಡ

Loose Talk

Words, like arrows cannot be retrieved.

ಬಿಟ್ಟ ಬಾಣ ಆಡಿದ ಮಾತು ಹಿಂದೆಬರದು.

Wounds inflicted by a sword will heal;
wounds inflicted by tongue don't heal.

ಶಸ್ತ್ರದಿಂದಾದ ಗಾಯ ಮಾಯುತ್ತದೆ,

ನಾಲಿಗೆಯಿಂದಾದ ಗಾಯ ಮಾಯುವುದಿಲ್ಲ.

Leaking pots spoil the stove, loose talks destroy the home.

ಮಡಿಕೆ ತೂತು ಒಲೆ ಕೆಡಿಸಿತು, ಹಗುರದ ಮಾತು ಮನೆ ಕೆಡಿಸಿತು.

A shameless tongue can fill your stomach.

ನಾಚಿಕೆ ಬಿಟ್ಟ ನಾಲಿಗೆ ಹೊಟ್ಟೆ ತುಂಬಿಸುತ್ತದೆ.

The boneless tongue will wag every which way.

ಎಲುಬಿಲ್ಲದ ನಾಲಿಗೆ ಹೇಗಾದರೂ ತಿರುಗುತ್ತದೆ.

Talk is charcoal, silence is gold.

ಮಾತು ಅಂಗಾರ, ಮೌನ ಬಂಗಾರ.

Love and Marriage

For a loving husband, even a monkey looks pretty.

ಕಟ್ಟಿಕೊಂಡವನಿಗೆ ಕೋಡಂಗಿಯೂ ಚಂದ.

Lust is blind.

ಕಾಮಕ್ಕೆ ಕಣ್ಣಿಲ್ಲ.

Conduct a marriage with a thousand lies.

ಸಾವಿರ ಸುಳ್ಳು ಹೇಳಿ ಒಂದು ಮದುವೆ ಮಾಡು.

Love cures animosity.

ವೈರತ್ವ ನಾಶಕ್ಕೆ ವಾತ್ಸಲ್ಯವೇ ಮದ್ದು.

Merchant

Where there is a merchant, there is a market.

ಶೆಟ್ಟಿ ಕೂತಲ್ಲೇ ಪಟ್ಟಣ.

A goldsmith cheats even on his sister.

ಅಕ್ಕಸಾಲಿ ಅಕ್ಕನ ಚಿನ್ನವನ್ನೂ ಕದಿಯದೆ ಬಿಡ.

Cheap merchant, stale corn.

ಅಗ್ಗದ ಶೆಟ್ಟಿ, ಮುಗಿದ ಜೋಳ.

Money Matters

Even a corpse smiles at the sound of money.

ಹಣ ಎಂದರೆ ಹೆಣವೂ ಬಾಯಿಕಳೆಯಿತು.

Money talks silently.

ದುಡ್ಡಿಗೆ ಸದ್ದಿಲ್ಲ.

A rich man has lots of relatives.

ಸಾಹುಕಾರನಿಗೆ ಬಳಗ ದೊಡ್ಡದು.

Wealth is like a cloud in summer—it floats away.

ಐಶ್ವರ್ಯ ಬರಗಾಲದ ಮೋಡದಂತೆ.

Debt is like a lancet around your neck kills.

సాలవే శూల.

ಸಾಲವೇ ಶೂಲ.

Tails follow bulls, debts follow weddings.

ಬಸವನ ಹಿಂದೆ ಬಾಲ ಲಗ್ನದ ಹಿಂದೆ ಸಾಲ.

Wealth and power pass like a dream.

ಧನ ಮತ್ತು ದೌಲತ್ತು ಕನಸಿನಂತೆ.

Hardship brings devotion. Wealth brings amnesia.

ಬಡತನದಲ್ಲಿ ಭಕ್ತಿ, ಸಿರಿತನದಲ್ಲಿ ಮರವು.

That rich man is my uncle.

ದುಡ್ಡಿದ್ದವನೇ ದೊಡ್ಡಪ್ಪ

Even junk discarded into the river must be weighed first. [5]

ಹೊಳೆಗೆ ಹಾಕಿದರೂ ಅಳೆದು ಹಾಕು.

The pie is only as good as its price.

ಕಾಸಿಗೆ ತಕ್ಕ ಕಜ್ಜಾಯ.

Wealth is fickle.

ಲಕ್ಷ್ಮಿ ಚಂಚಲೆ.

Even a flower offered to a poor God frowned at him.

ಬಡವ ದೇವರ ಕಂಡರೆ ಬಿಲ್ವ ಪತ್ರೆ ಬುಸ್ಸಂತು.

Mother

Even the king has a mother.

ರಾಜನಿಗೂ ಒಬ್ಬ ತಾಯಿ.

Nothing is tastier than salt, no one is dearer than mother.

ಉಪ್ಪಿಗಿಂತ ರುಚಿಇಲ್ಲ, ತಾಯಿಗಿಂತ ಬಂಧುವಿಲ್ಲ.

A mother's embrace shelters [you] like the shade of a banyan tree.

ತಾಯಿಯ ಮಡಿಲು ಹೊಂಗೆಯ ನೆರಳು.

A motherless home is like a treeless jungle.

ತಾಯಿಇಲ್ಲದ ಮನೆ ಗಿಡವಿಲ್ಲದ ಕಾಡು.

A plant never feels that its melon is heavy.

ಬಳ್ಳಿಗೆ ಕಾಯಿ ಭಾರವೇ?

The road to my mother's house is always smooth and has no thorns. [6]

ತವರೂರ ದಾರಿಯಲಿ ಕಲ್ಲಿಲ್ಲ ಮುಳ್ಳಿಲ್ಲ.

After mother's death, the father is an uncle.

ಅವ್ವ ಸತ್ತಮೇಲೆ ಅಪ್ಪ ಚಿಕ್ಕಪ್ಪ.

Instead of praying ten gods, pray one mother.

ಹತ್ತು ದೇವರನ್ನು ಪೂಜಿಸುವ ಬದಲು ಹೆತ್ತ
ತಾಯಿಯನ್ನು ಮೂಜಿಸು

Mothers-In-Law

The pot the mother-in-law broke was not expensive.

ಅತ್ತೆ ಒಡೆದ ಮಡಿಕೆಗೆ ಬೆಲೆಇಲ್ಲ.

Mother-in-law never loves her daughter-in-law.

ಅತ್ತೆ ಎಂದೂ ಸೊಸೆಯನ್ನು ಪ್ರೀತಿಸಳು.

[One should have] a mother like a pearl, mother-in-law like a mule.

ಮುತ್ತಿನಂಥಾ ತಾಯಿ, ಕತ್ತೆಯಂಥಾ ಅತ್ತೆ.

Six months after mother- in-law died, the daughter-in-law cried.

ಅತ್ತೆ ಸತ್ತು ಆರು ತಿಂಗಳ ಮೇಲೆ ಸೊಸೆಯ ಕಣ್ಣಲ್ಲಿ ನೀರು ಬಂತು.

Obvious Mistakes

Like falling during the day into a well
you clearly saw at midnight.

ನಡುರಾತ್ರಿಯಲ್ಲಿ ನೋಡಿದ ಬಾವಿಗೆ ಹಗಲಲ್ಲಿ
ಬಿದ್ದಂತೆ.

Like sticking one's finger in a pot of boiling water.

ಕುದಿಯುವ ನೀರಲ್ಲಿ ಬೆರಳದ್ದಿದ ಹಾಗೆ.

Don't hire a wolf to guard your sheep.

ಕುರಿ ಕಾಯೋದಕ್ಕೆ ತೋಳನನ್ನು ಕಳಿಸಿದರಂತೆ

Obvious Truth

The crowd is crazy; a county fair is insane.

ಜನ ಮರುಳೋ ಜಾತ್ರೆ ಮರುಳೋ.

You don't need a mirror to see a blister on the palm.

ಅಂಗೈ ಹುಣ್ಣ ನೋಡಲು ಕನ್ನಡಿ ಏಕೆ?

Cat drinks the stolen milk with closed eyes [yet all can see].

ಬೆಕ್ಕು ಕಣ್ಣು ಮುಚ್ಚಿಕೊಂಡು ಹಾಲು ಕುಡಿದರೆ
ಯಾರಿಗೂ ಕಾಣುವುದಿಲ್ಲವೇ?

A son-in-law's blindness is revealed at dawn.

ಅಳಿಯನ ಕುರುಡು ಬೆಳಗಾದರೆ ಕಂಡೀತು.

Even in *Kaashi* the chair has only four legs. ⸗

ಕಾಶಿಯಲ್ಲೂ ಕುರ್ಚಿಗೆ ನಾಲ್ಕೇ ಕಾಲು.

The grass does not grow where ten people walk.

ಹಾತ್ತು ಜನ ನಡೆಯುವಲ್ಲಿ ಹುಲ್ಲು ಬೆಳೆಯದು.

One of a Kind

Cunning teacher, rascal disciple

ಚೋರ ಗುರು, ಚಂಡಾಲ ಶಿಷ್ಯ.

As is the thread, so is the sari.

ನೂಲಿನಂತೆ ಸೀರೆ.

Pain/Pleasure

No thorns no roses, no pain no labor.

ಮುಳ್ಳಿಲ್ಲದೆ ಗುಲಾಬಿ ಇಲ್ಲ, ನೋವಿಲ್ಲದೆ ಹೆರಿಗೆಯಿಲ್ಲ.

Paradox (Catch 22)

The protective fence ate away the crops.

ಬೇಲಿ ಎದ್ದು ಹೊಲ ಮೈದಂತೆ.

Without knowing how to swim, one must not dive in the lake; without diving, one cannot learn to swim.

ಈಜು ಬರದ ಹೊರತು ನೀರಿಗಿಳಿಯ ಬಾರದು;
ನೀರಿಗಿಳಿಯದ ಹೊರತು ಈಜು ಬಾರದು.

Marriage cures madness— madness prevents marriage.

ಹುಚ್ಚು ಹೋಗದೇ ಮದುವೆಯಾಗದು,
ಮದುವೆಯಾಗದೇ ಹುಚ್ಚು ಹೋಗದು.

[He has] No feathers, no beaks, yet they call him Mr. Bird.

ರೆಕ್ಕೆ ಇಲ್ಲ, ಕೊಕ್ಕಿಲ್ಲ, ಹೆಸರು ಗರುಡಯ್ಯಂಗಾರ್ರು.

Perspective

Cat's Game, rat's death.

ಬೆಕ್ಕಿಗೆ ಆಟ ಇಲಿಗೆ ಪ್ರಾಣ ಸಂಕಟ.

Even rat pups are pretty to rat moms.

ಹೆತ್ತವಳಿಗೆ ಹೆಗ್ಗಣ ಮುದ್ದು.

A drowning man cannot worry about getting wet from the rain.

ನೀರಿನಲ್ಲಿ ಮುಳುಗಿದವನಿಗೆ ಚಳಿಏನು ಗಾಳಿಏನು?

Where there is fire, there is light.

ಬೆಂಕಿ ಇದ್ದಲ್ಲಿ ಬೆಳಕೂ ಇರುತದೆ.

Quarreling with a perfume salesman is better than romancing a garbage collector.

ಸಗಣಿ ತೆಗೆಯುವವನ ಜತೆ ಸರಸಕ್ಕಿಂತ ಗಂಧಮಾರುವವನ ಜತೆ ಗುದ್ದಾಟವೇ ಲೇಸು.

A dispute with a scholar is better than a friendship with a scoundrel.

ಚಂಡಾಲನೊಡನೆ ಸ್ನೇಹಕ್ಕಿಂತ ಪಂಡಿತನೊಡನೆ ಜಗಳವೇ ಮೇಲು.

If my neighbor's house is ruined, I can build a barn there.

ಪಕ್ಕದ ಮನೆ ಬಿದ್ರೆ ಕರು ಕಟ್ಟೋಕೆ ಜಾಗ ಆಯ್ತು.

An enemy nearby is better than a friend far away.

ದೂರದ ಮಿತ್ರನಿಗಿಂತ ಹತ್ತಿರದ ಶತ್ರು ಮೇಲು.

After crossing the river, the boatman is my lover.

ಹೊಳೆ ದಾಟಿದ ಮೇಲೆ ಅಂಬಿಗನು ಮಿಂಡ.

Poet

A poet can see what even the sun cannot.

ರವಿ ಕಾಣದ್ದನ್ನು ಕವಿ ಕಂಡ.

Precarious

A lamp on a cat's head will surely fall.

ಬೆಕ್ಕಿನ ತಲೆಯಮೇಲೆ ದೀಪವಿಟ್ಟಂತೆ.

A lamp on a slanted wall cannot stay long.

ಅಡ್ಡ ಗೋಡೆಯ ಮೇಲೆ ದೀಪವಿಟ್ಟಂತೆ.

Pride/False

Little knowledge, lots of pride.

ಅಲ್ಪವಿದ್ಯಾ ಮಹಾ ಗರ್ವಿ.

A tall tree must know that there are taller ones.

ಮರಕ್ಕೆ ಮತ್ತೊಂದು ಮರ ಎತ್ತರ.

I may be down [in a wrestling match], but there is no dust on my mustache.

ನೆಲಕ್ಕೆ ಬಿದ್ದರೂ ಮೀಸೆ ಮಣ್ಣಾಗಲಿಲ್ಲ.

For every strong man there is one stronger.

ಒಬ್ಬ ಜಟ್ಟಿಗಿಂತ ಮತ್ತೊಬ್ಬ ಗಟ್ಟಿ.

Ignoring the vain cures his pride.

ಅಹಂಕಾರಕ್ಕೆ ಉದಾಸೀನವೆ ಮದ್ದು.

Proverb

Proverbs and the Vedas are alike.[8]

ಗಾದೆ ವೇದಕ್ಕೆ ಸಮ.

The Vedas may lie. Proverbs don't.

ವೇದ ಸುಳ್ಳಾದರೂ ಗಾದೆ ಸುಳ್ಳಾಗದು.

What doesn't exist in the Vedas can be found in proverbs.

ವೇದದಲ್ಲಿಲ್ಲದ್ದು ಗಾದೆಯಲ್ಲಿರುತ್ತದೆ.

The people's voice is God's voice.

ಜನತೆಯ ಮಾತು ಜನಾರ್ಧನನ ಮಾತು.

A proverb in your speech is like chutney with your rice.

ಮಾತಿನಲ್ಲಿ ಗಾದೆ, ಊಟದಲ್ಲಿ ಉಪ್ಪಿನ ಕಾಯಿ.

A proverb omitted in talk is like the romance omitted in love.

ಗಾದೆಯಿಲ್ಲದ ಮಾತು ಸರಸವಿಲ್ಲದ ಪ್ರೀತಿಯಂತೆ.

Relationship

Wounds heal; scars don't.

ಗಾಯ ಮಾದರೂ ಕಲೆ ಹೋಗದು.

A broken house can be rebuilt—not a broken heart.

ಮುರಿದ ಮನೆ ಕಟ್ಟಬಹುದು, ಒಡೆದ ಮನ ಕಟ್ಟಲಾಗದು.

Relatives/Sons/Children

Beget a son, plant a coconut tree and prosper. 9

ಗಂಡು ಹೆರು, ತೆಂಗು ನಡು..

When I have a baby on my shoulders, why should I bother about the heavens?

ಕಂಕುಳಲ್ಲಿ ಕೂಸಿದ್ದ ಮ್ಯಾಗೆ ಕೈಲಾಸದ ಚಿಂತೆ ನನಗ್ಯಾಕೆ?

Siblings at birth turn into [quarreling] cousins when grown up.[10]

ಹುಟ್ಟಿದಾಗ ಅಣ್ಣ ತಮ್ಮ, ಬೆಳೆದಮೇಲೆ ದಾಯಾದಿಗಳು.

The brother is ours, not the sister-in-law.

ಅಣ್ಣ ನಮ್ಮವನು, ಅತ್ತಿಗೆ ನಮ್ಮವಳಲ್ಲ.

The brother-in-law is a relative only if the sister is alive.

ಅಕ್ಕ ಇದ್ದರೇ ಭಾವ.

Relative Value

A lone survivor in a ruined town is the sheriff.

ಹಾಳೂರಿಗೆ ಉಳಿದವನೇ ಗೌಡ.

Piglets are plenty; lion pups are few.

ಹಂದಿಗೆ ಹಲವು ಮರಿಗಳು, ಸಿಂಹಕ್ಕೆ ಒಂದೇ ಮರಿ.

In the land of the nose-less people, the one with the nose is ugly.

ಮೂಗಿಲ್ಲದೂರಿನಲ್ಲಿ ಮೂಗುಳ್ಳವನೇ ಕುರೂಪಿ.

What took a year for the potter, took a minute for the cane [to break the pot].

ಕುಂಬಾರನಿಗೆ ವರುಷ, ದೊಣ್ಣೆಗೆ ನಿಮಿಷ.

Responsibility

The elephant carries the elephant-weight.
The ant carries an ant's burden.

ಆನೆಯ ಭಾರ ಆನೆಗೆ, ಇರುವೆಯ ಭಾರ ಇರುವೆಗೆ.

I am the boss; you are the chief; who is
going to row the boat?

ನಾನೂ ನಾಯಕ, ನೀನೂ ನಾಯಕ, ದೋಣಿ

ಒತ್ತುವವನು ಯಾರು?

127

Rich/poor

A rich man has relatives all over town.

ಬಕ್ಕಳ ಹೊನ್ನಿದ್ದರೆ ಊರೆಲ್ಲಾ ನೆಂಟರು.

Wealth of a brainless man is like a horse without reins.

ಬುದ್ಧಿಇಲ್ಲದವನ ಐಶ್ವರ್ಯ ಕಡಿವಾಣವಿಲ್ಲದ ಕುದುರೆಯಂತೆ.

A person with no money is worse than a corpse.

ಹಣವಿಲ್ಲದವನು ಹೆಣಕ್ಕಿಂತ ಕಡೆ.

When a poor man makes a mistake, we call it deception; when a rick man makes a mistake, we call it profit.

ಬಡವ ಮಾಡಿದರೆ ಅನ್ಯಾಯ, ಬಲ್ಲಿದ ಮಾಡಿದರೆ ಆದಾಯ.

Saints and Sinners

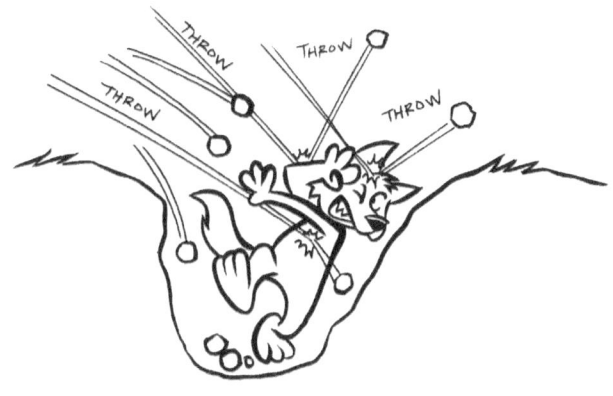

When a fox is trapped in the ditch, everyone throws stones.

ತೋಳ ಹೊಂದಕ್ಕೆ ಬಿದ್ದರೆ ಆಳಿಗೊಂದು ಕಲ್ಲು.

When a sinner dives, even the ocean dries up.

ಪಾಪಿ ಸಮುದ್ರಕ್ಕೆ ಹೋದರೆ ಮೊಳಕಾಲುದ್ದ ನೀರು.

Washing the skin doesn't wash the sin.

ಚರ್ಮ ತೊಳೆದರೆ ಕರ್ಮ ಹೋದೀತೇ?

Judge a saint in the manner of his death.

ಶರಣರ ಗುಣ ಮರಣದಲ್ಲಿ ನೋಡು.

Don't look for a river's origin or a saint's past.

ನದೀ ಮೂಲ, ಖುಷೀ ಮೂಲ ಹುಡುಕಬೇಡ.

The sword-maker should not share the sins of the butcher.

ಕೊಡಲಿ ಮಾಡಿದವನಿಗೆ ಕೊಲೆಗಡುಕನ ಪಾಪ ಬರದು.

A thief's wife is forever a widow.

ಕಳ್ಳನ ಹೆಂಡತಿ ಎಂದಿದ್ದರೂ ಮುಂಡೆ.

Stay away from saints and prostitutes.

ಸನ್ಯಾಸಿಯ ಬಳಿ ಸೂಳೆಯ ಬಳಿ ಸುಳಿಯಬೇಡ.

Self-self-awareness (lack of)

Rosary pea does not know its butt is black.

ಗುಲಗಂಜಿಗೆ ತನ್ನ ತಿಕದ ಕಪ್ಪು ಕಾಣದು.

Shallow Philosophy

When there is famine, I wish for nothing.

ಬರಗಾಲದಲ್ಲಿ ನನಗೇನೂ ಬೇಡ.

An aging woman remains chaste.

ವೃದ್ಧನಾರೀ ಪತಿವ್ರತೆ.

Shame/Honor

A thief's shame cannot be erased by (his) donating an elephant.

ಅಡಿಕೆ ಕದ್ದ ಅವಮಾನ ಆನೆ ಕೊಟ್ಟರೂ ಹೋಗದು.

Short Memories

Dead cows gave tons of milk.

ಸತ್ತ ಮ್ಮೈಗೆ ಹತ್ತು ಸೇರು ಹಾಲು.

After the rain, the umbrella feels heavy.

ಮಳೆ ನಿಂತ ಮೇಲೆ ಕೊಡೆ ಭಾರ.

When your stomach is full, even the maple syrup tastes bitter.

ಹೊಟ್ಟೆ ತುಂಬಿದ ಮೇಲೆ ಕಜ್ಜಾಯ ವಿಷ.

Strength

Tactics are better than brute force.

ಶಕ್ತಿಗಿಂತ ಯುಕ್ತಿ ಮೇಲು.

Surprise

It was as if a tiger delivered a hyena.

ಹುಲಿಗೆ ನರಿ ಹುಟ್ಟಿದಂತೆ.

Thief/Theft

Only a thief knows a thief's footmarks.

ಕಳ್ಳನ ಹೆಜ್ಜೆ ಕಳ್ಳನೇ ಬಲ್ಲ.

Tight Spots (indecision)

Between a cliff and a tiger.

ಅತ್ತ ದಾರಿ ಇತ್ತ ಪುಲಿ.

Fearing the tiger, would you jump in the river?

ಹುಲಿಗೆ ಹೆದರಿ ನದಿಗೆ ಹಾರುವರೇ.

No more than six, no less than three [neither less nor more].

ಆರಕ್ಕೆ ಹೆಚ್ಚಿಲ್ಲ, ಮೂರಕ್ಕೆ ಕಮ್ಮಿ ಇಲ್ಲ.

The snake must not die; the stick must not break.[11]

ಹಾವೂ ಸಾಯಬಾರದು, ಕೋಲೂ
ಮುರಿಯಬಾರದು.

Time

Shower water reaches the feet, too.

ತಲೆಗೆ ಬಿದ್ದ ನೀರು ಕಾಲಿಗೂ ಬರುತ್ತದೆ.

Like a flower, beauty also fades.

ಹೂವಿನಂತೆ ರೂಪವೂ ಬಾಡುತ್ತದೆ.

Timeliness

Don't start digging for water when the house is on fire.

ಮನೆ ಉರಿಯುವಾಗ ಬಾವಿತೋಡಿದರಂತೆ.

Don't start battle drills when the war begins.

ಯುದ್ಧಕಾಲೇ ಶಸ್ತ್ರಾಬ್ಯಾಸ.

A good deed must be carried out immediately.

ಶುಭಸ್ಯ ಶೀಘ್ರಂ.

Uncertain Future

Troops march in and battles may rage—
eat your soup, my son!

ಪೌಜು ಬಂದೀತು, ಕದನ ನಡೆದೀತು, ನಿನ್ನೂಟ
ಮುಗಿಸು ಮಗನೇ!

Virtue/Lack of Virtue

Being kind is being good.

ಔದಾರ್ಯವೇ ಸುಗುಣ.

Smiling is heaven.

ನಕ್ಕರದೇ ಸ್ವರ್ಗ.

A pitcher filled with water doesn't spill.

ತುಂಬಿದ ಕೊಡ ತುಳುಕುವುದಿಲ್ಲ

A lack of virtue shows like a protruding tooth.

ದುರ್ಗುಣ ಕೋರೆಹಲ್ಲಿನಂತೆ. .

Sandalwood, the more you grind it, the better it smells.

ಗಂಧ ತೀವಿದಷ್ಟೂ ಸುವಾಸನೆ.

Extreme politeness is the sign of a rascal.

ಆತಿವಿನಯಂ ಧೂರ್ತ ಲಕ್ಷಣಂ.

Never deceive the one who fed you the salt (i.e., the one who fed you).

ಉಪ್ಪುಂಡ ಮಗೆಗೆ ಎರಡು ಬಗೆಯಬೇಡ.

The longer you boil the milk, the better it tastes.

ಹಾಲು ಕುದಿದಷ್ಟೂ ರುಚಿ ಜಾಸ್ತಿ.

A gift given is yours. A wealth hoarded is for others.

ಕೊಟ್ಟದ್ದು ತನಗೆ ಬಚ್ಚಿಟ್ಟದ್ದು ಪರರಿಗೆ.

Truth doesn't die, lies don't win.

ಸತ್ಯಕ್ಕೆ ಸಾವಿಲ್ಲ, ಸುಳ್ಳಿಗೆ ಜಯವಿಲ್ಲ.

War and Peace

Peace has no vice. War has no virtue.

ಶಾಂತಿಗೆ ದೋಷವಿಲ್ಲ, ಯುದ್ಧಕ್ಕೆ ಗುಣವಿಲ್ಲ.

All soldiers are brave before the battle begins.

ಯುದ್ಧಕ್ಕೆ ಮುಂಚೆ ಎಲ್ಲ ಸಿಪಾಯಿಗಳೂ ಶೂರರೇ!

A soldier's wife is forever a widow.

ಸಿಪಾಯಿಯ ಹೆಂಡತಿ ಎಂದಿಗೂ ವಿಧವೆ.

When two people quarrel, the third person profits.

ಇಬ್ಬರ ಜಗಳದಲ್ಲಿ ಮೂರನೆಯವನಿಗೆ ಲಾಭ.

Waste / Wasteful Deeds

A mirror is useless for a blind man.

ಕುರುಡನ ಕೈಗೆ ಕನ್ನಡಿ ಏಕೆ?

Don't play the flute to please a buffalo.

ಕೋಣನ ಮುಂದೆ ಕಿನ್ನರಿ ಬಾರಿಸುವರೇ?

Why do you stitch a pair of pants for the elephant?[12]

ಆನೆಗೆ ಚಡ್ಡಿಯಾಕೆ ಹೊಲಿಸುತ್ತೀ?

155

Do not haul stone to the hill.

ಬೆಟ್ಟಕ್ಕೆ ಕಲ್ಲು ಹೊತ್ತ ಹಾಗೆ.

Like climbing a ladder to reach for the skies.

ಆಕಾಷಕ್ಕೆ ಏಣಿ ಹಾಕಿದ ಹಾಗೆ.

The rainwater falling on a boulder is simply wasted.

ಭೋರ್ಗಲ್ಲ ಮೇಲೆ ಮಳೆ ಸುರಿದಂತೆ.

You will hurt yourself by beating the wind.

ಗಾಳಿಯನ್ನು ಗುದ್ದಿ ಮೈನೋಯಿಸಿಕೊಂಡ ಹಾಗೆ.

Wife / Women / Man

Share love with your wife, secrets with your mother.

ಹೆಂಡತಿಗೆ ಪ್ರೇಮ ಕೊಡು, ತಾಯಿಗೆ ಗುಟ್ಟು
ಕೊಡು.

A call girl has eighteen names.

ಹಾದರಗಿತ್ತಿಗೆ ಹದಿನೆಂಟು ಹೆಸರು.

Don't trust a woman with instant tears and a man with instant smiles.

ಅಳುವ ಹೆಣ್ಣನ್ನೂ ನಗುವ ಗಂಡನ್ನೂ ನಂಬಬೇಡ.

A home with no wife, a lute with no string, and a temple with no God are all the same.

ಮಡದಿ ಇಲ್ಲದ ಮನೆ, ತಂತಿ ಇಲ್ಲದ ವೀಣೆ,
ದೇವರಿಲ್ಲದ ದೇಗುಲ, ಎಲ್ಲಾ ಒಂದೇ.

The home without a woman is like a town without water.

ನಾರಿ ಇಲ್ಲದ ಮನೆ ನೀರಿಲ್ಲದ ಊರಿನಂತೆ.

Beware of the wife who is too pretty.

ಭಾರ್ಯಾ ರೂಪವತಿ ಶತ್ರುಃ

If there is money, there is a concubine.

ಧನವಿದ್ದಲ್ಲಿ ಸೂಳೆ.

Call girls and smallpox have neither scruples nor pity.

ಸಿಡುಬಿಗೂ ಸೂಳೆಗೂ ಕರುಣೆಯಿಲ್ಲ, ಬೇಧವಿಲ್ಲ.

Men don't hold babies; women don't
hold secrets.

ಗಂಡಸರ ಕೈಯಲ್ಲಿ ಕೂಸು ನಿಲ್ಲದು, ಹೆಂಗಸರ
ಬಾಯಲ್ಲಿ ಮಾತು ನಿಲ್ಲದು.

Fire is an angry woman.

ನಾರಿ ಉರಿಯುವ ಮಾರಿ.

An angry woman is an angry goddess.

ನಾರಿ, ಮುನಿದರೆ ಮಾರಿ.

Winning

Mine is the winner's side.

ನಾನು ಗೆದ್ದವನ ಕಡೆ.

My victory is from my efforts—my loss, God's wish.

ಗೆದ್ದರೆ ನನ್ನ ಪ್ರಯತ್ನದಿಂದ, ಸೋತರೆ ದೈವೇಚ್ಛೆ.

Like hanging on to the tail of the winning horse.

ಗೆದ್ದೆತ್ತಿನ ಬಾಲ ಹಿಡಿದ ಹಾಗೆ.

163

Worth (lack of)

A dog on the throne [leads the country to ruins].

ನಾಯಿ ಸಿಂಹಾಸನದ ಮೇಲೆ ಕೂತಂತೆ.

Homegrown shrub is not medicine-worthy.

ಹಿತ್ತಲ ಗಿಡ ಮದ್ದಲ್ಲ.

Appendix

Proverbs and similes are often used in conversation with little distinction. Sometimes a proverb may function as a simile; for instance, one may say, "This elected official is like a dog on the throne." In this collection, I have therefore retained a few popular similes.

Many proverbs reflect more than one meaning. Yet, somewhat reluctantly, I have classified the proverbs into arbitrary categories to maintain a structural format. Categorizing proverbs helps readers understand their context and meaning.

1. Our village monkey is a king in the city, poking fun at the notion that village folks are simpletons. The proverb reminds us that, for all their apparent sophistication, the city people may even crown a monkey as their king, a monkey clearly seen by the villagers!

2. My apologies to short people and to those with red hair or green (or gray) eyes for including the following two proverbs: "Even if you trust a thief, don't trust a dwarf," and "Beware of [people with] red hair or cat's eyes." Clearly these are inappropriate and insulting a segment of our population. However, their cultural context makes them interesting and funny.

Dwarves are rare, as are those with red hair or blue-gray eyes (the latter), especially in India. These proverbs highlight prejudices against people with rare traits, unusual features, or who 'just look slightly different.' Such prejudices are common in other cultures.

Suggesting an 'untrustworthy nature' for the dwarves may have begun with circus clowns who engage in tricks and buffoonery; however, this is an unjust stereotype. A similar reference to the red-haired and 'cat's-eyed' persons may reflect an indignant attitude towards the Europeans who colonized India and ruled it for centuries.

3. Grandparents occupy a unique place in all Asian cultures. They are the symbols of stability, a source of love and wisdom, and of course, an irritation that must be endured (at least sometimes). Of the many proverbs on grandparents, I have included only two in this collection.

In grandmothers know how to cough, the youngsters are reminded about their grandmothers' long experiences with such ordinary 'tasks' as coughing. Grandmothers are often sick too.

4. There is a fantastic episode in the Aranya Parva (The Book of the Forest) section of the great Indian epic, The Mahabharata. An invisible spirit challenges the exiled king Dharmaraya to answer a series of questions; failing to do so, Dharmaraya would die. To one question, "What is grief?" the wise Dharmaraya answers, "Ignorance is grief." Contrast this to the well-known English proverb, "Ignorance is bliss."

5. The Kannada original proverb goes: "Even the junk discarded into the river must be weighed first." The ritual of offering food, money, or other valuables into the river has been in practice for centuries during religious ceremonies or holy occasions. The pragmatic-minded, however, may choose to drop only unwanted junk. This mischievously reinforces the value of such a practical-minded approach.

6. A daughter's attachment to her mother's house never fades. The first homecoming after marriage is especially precious, which conjures up tremendous emotions in the Indian psyche. The proverb "The road to my mother's house is always smooth and has no thorns" declares that no obstacle will keep the daughter from making such a sentimental trip.

7. Kaashi [Benares, now Varanasi] is the ultimate holy city for Hindus. The orthodox believe that all auspicious ceremonies must be carried out in Kaashi because it is a special place. The proverb, even in Kaashi, a chair has only four legs, mocks that all may not be holy or special there. Even in Kaashi, everyday objects remain common.

8. The Vedas are the most ancient of Hindu scriptures. The Rig Veda is followed in approximate chronological order by Yajur Veda, Sama Veda, and Atharvana Veda. Comparing proverbs to the Vedas is a powerful affirmation of their authenticity, endurance, and preciousness.

9. The coconut has an essential place in Indian life. Its pulp and oil are used in cooking. It is offered in religious ceremonies and given as a gift on auspicious occasions. From the coconut tree, one can produce ropes, build boats and huts, and make roofing materials. Thus, the proverb, "Beget a son, plant a coconut tree and prosper" alludes to the lasting value of the coconut.

There is also the age-old 'male bias' reflected in this proverb. As in Chinese and other ancient cultures, there are literally hundreds of proverbs proclaiming the 'misfortune' and 'liability' of having a daughter, and the 'luck' and 'value' of begetting a son. Of course, other proverbs also praise the virtues of being a woman. Thankfully, the traditional 'male bias' is fading. With an improving economy and education, a more balanced outlook towards children of either sex has emerged in many sectors of modern India.

10. The proverb, siblings at birth turn into quarreling cousins when grown up, suggests that even close brothers and sisters may fight for their share of inheritance later in life. The proverb is also a tangential reference to the central story of The Mahabharata, in which the war of succession between the Pandava and Kaurava cousins led to a near-total destruction.

11. The fear of snakes is universal. Hindus worship the likeness of cobras. The scriptures forbid cobra killings, but such killings are common. The proverb "The snake must not die; the stick should not break." dramatizes the conflict between the fear of snakes and the taboo on killing them. You may pretend to beat the cobra to death; yet you don't break the stick or kill the snake—so, no sin is committed.

12. Elephants are highly regarded animals in Indian life. Elaborately decorated elephants are taken into procession during religious festivals or in royal ceremonies. The proverb, "Don't stitch a pair of pants for the elephant," makes fun of the futility of undertaking meaningless practices to extremes.

Bibliography

1. Manasa and Manjula Manasa. Janapriya Saaviraaru
   GaadhegaLu (A Thousand Popular Proverbs), Tanu
   Mana Prakashana, Mysore, India, 1999.

2. A. K. Ramanujan. GaadhegaLu (Proverbs) Karnataka
   University, Dharwar, India, 1955.

3. Dr. Rame Gowda. Kittel KOshadha GaadhegaLu
   (Proverbs of the Kittel Dictionary, 3rd Edition) D.V.K.
   Murthy, Publishers, Mysore, India 1998.

4. Dr. Rame Gowda. Namma GaadhegaLu (Our Proverbs,
   4th Edition.) Geetha Book House Publishers, Mysore,
   India, 1994.

5. A. R. Satish Hegde and K. Rangachari. Janapriya
   GaadhegaLu (Popular Proverbs) Gayathri Prakashana,
   Bangalore, India, 1998.

6. H. C. Shanthaveeraiah and H. S. Muththishree
   GaadhegaLa Saagara (An Ocean of Proverbs) Vasana
   Book Depot, Bangalore, India. 1995.

7. T.V. Venkataramanaiah. Kannada GaadhegaLa KOsha (A
   Dictionary of Kannada Proverbs) Pratibha Granthamaala,
   Dharwar, India,1963.

The Author

Tonse Narayana Krishna Raju, MD, is a physician, researcher, and medical historian with a distinguished career in neonatology and pediatrics. Previously, he served as a professor of Pediatrics at the University of Illinois in Chicago and now serves as a scientist at the National Institutes of Health. Besides authoring more than 200 scientific articles, he is the author of five books of fiction.

His other books include: *The Importance of Having a Brain: Tales from the History of Medicine, Second Edition* and *Nobel Chronicles: A Handbook of Nobel Prizes in Physiology or Medicine, 1901—2004 Second Edition* (both by Auctorem House and Boundless Book Publishers).Dr. Raju and his wife reside in Gaithersburg, Maryland.

The Artist

Arthur Baltazar, a freelance cartoonist, studied art at Columbia College, Chicago. He created the comic book series, *Patrick the Wolf Boy*, and has produced children's books for Warner Brothers Studios. Mr. Baltazar lives in Chicago and runs the *Electric Milk Creations* art studio.